LET ME TELL YOU THE Q4 STORY OF AEW IN 2024 TO BEGIN YOUR 2025

ALL ELITE WRESTLING ALL OUT, WRESTLEDREAM, AND FULL GEAR EVENTS ALL AT A GO (SEPTEMBER, OCTOBER AND NOVEMBER)

All rights reserved. No part of this publication may be reproduced, distributed, or transmitted in any form or by any means, including photocopying, recording, or other electronic or mechanical methods, without the prior written permission of the publisher, except in the case of brief quotations embodied in critical reviews and certain other noncommercial uses permitted by copyright law.

© Jack Vale, 2024.

About the Author

I'm Jack Vale, an independent publisher and resident trend compiler with a lifelong passion for professional wrestling. This book is a deep dive into the most electrifying quarter of AEW in 2024, capturing the raw energy and unforgettable moments from All Out, WrestleDream, and Full Gear.

I'm not just another wrestling writer; I'm a fan who lives and breathes this sport. I feel the electric crackle before every major bout, the gasp-inducing impact of every near fall, and the exhilaration of a perfectly executed moonsault. Every drop of sweat, every roar from the crowd – it all tells a story, and I bring it to life on the page.

Inside, you'll find:
- Ringside Analysis: Experience the most memorable confrontations, jaw-dropping moments, and the rise of new stars that ignited AEW's already blazing fire.
- Unfiltered Passion: This isn't just a recap; it's a love letter to the drama, athleticism, and pure, unadulterated entertainment that makes AEW so special.
- A Fan's Perspective: I'm deeply rooted in the wrestling community, sharing insights and observations with fellow fans while constantly searching for the next big thing.

Whether you're a seasoned wrestling veteran or just starting to explore the world of AEW, this book will give you a front-row seat to the most spectacular quarter in the company's history.

Let me tell you the Q4 story of AEW in 2024 and begin your 2025 with a bang.

Connect with me:

https://www.amazon.com/author/jackvale

Let's discuss wrestling, share our passion, and keep the spirit of this incredible sport alive.

TABLE OF CONTENTS

CHAPTER ONE
All Out 2024: The Battle for Glory
The Road to All Out
The Matches Begin
The Main Show
The Climactic Steel Cage Match
Results

CHAPTER TWO
Wrestle-Dream 2024: A Night of Triumph and Heartbreak
The Road to Wrestle-Dream
The Night Begins: Zero Hour
The Main Show: High Stakes and Unforgettable Moments
The Ultimate Climax: Title Matches and Career-Defining Moments
The Ultimate Victory
Results

CHAPTER THREE
Full Gear 2024: The Ultimate Showdown
The Road to Full Gear
Zero Hour: The Pre-show Action
Main Show: High Stakes and Epic Feuds
The Main Event: MJF vs. Roderick Strong
Results

CHAPTER FOUR
AEW Women's World Championship
History
Belt Design
Reigns
Cumulative Reigns

CHAPTER FIVE
AEW World Championship
History
"Real World Championship"
Belt Design
Custom Designs
Reigns

CHAPTER SIX
AEW International Championship
History
Belt Design
Reigns
Legacy

CHAPTER SEVEN
AEW TBS Championship
History
The TBS Championship Tournament
Belt Design
Reigns
Legacy

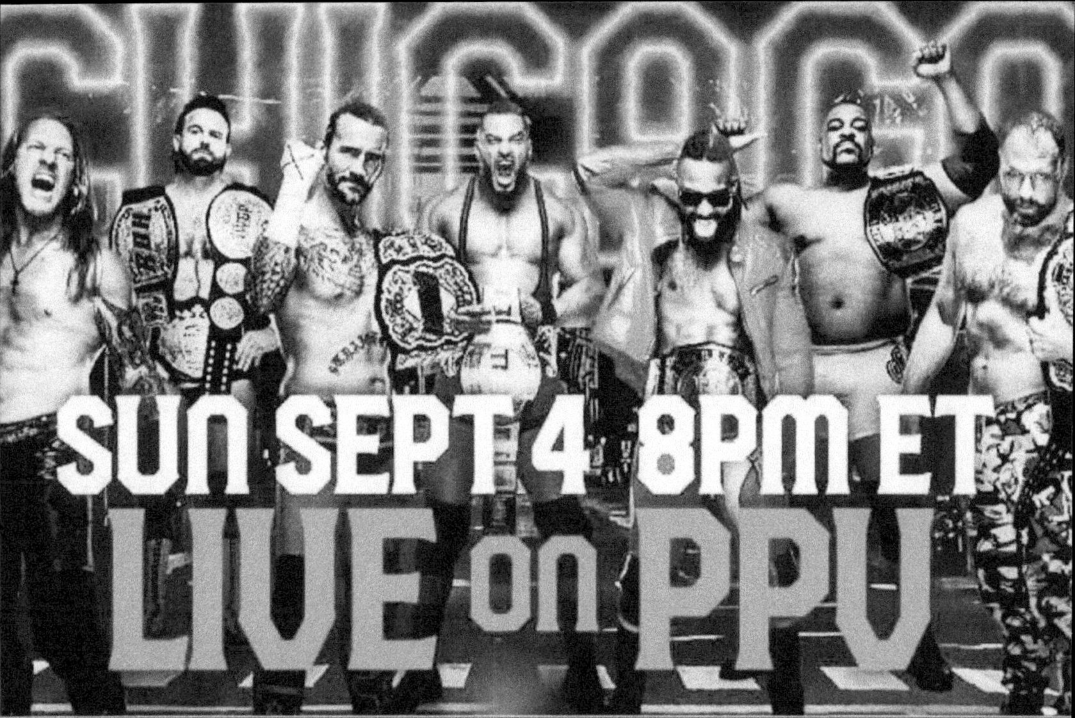
SUN SEPT 4 8PM ET
LIVE on PPV

CHAPTER ONE

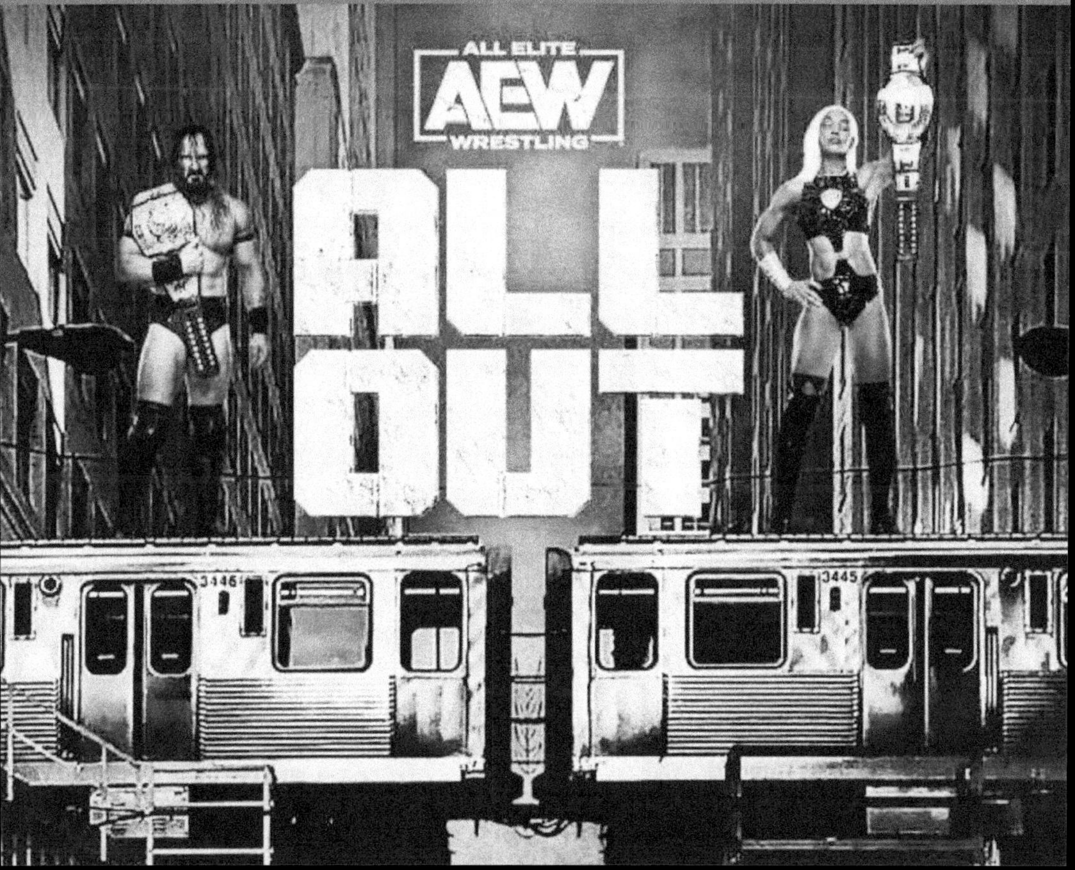
ALL ELITE
AEW
WRESTLING
ALL
OUT
3446
3445

CHAPTER ONE
All Out 2024: The Battle for Glory

All Out 2024: The Battle for Glory

On September 7, 2024, All Elite Wrestling (AEW) hosted its Pay Per View extravaganza, All Out 2024, at the Now Arena in Hoffman Estates, a suburb of Chicago, Illinois. The crowd had been buzzing all week, not only because this was the sixth edition of AEW's legendary All Out pay-per-view but also because this event had the spotlight for another monumental reason. For the first time since 2020, the event would take place on a Saturday night, after a fan-driven decision to push back the date a week due to the original Sunday timing, which came dangerously close to AEW's previous event, All In, held just a week earlier.

The Now Arena, a familiar battleground for AEW fans, had witnessed many great moments in wrestling history. The crowd had witnessed it all: from breathtaking flips to fierce rivalries, and this year's event promised even more than anyone had expected.

The Road to All Out

Before the night unfolded, the storylines had been brewing on AEW's flagship programs—Dynamite, Collision, and Rampage. Wrestling is always about the build, and AEW delivered it in spades this year. Feuds weren't just about the in-ring action—they were about redemption, unfinished business, and the chance to claim ultimate glory.

In one of the most personal rivalries, "Hangman" Adam Page and Swerve Strickland had been feuding for nearly a year.

What began as a competitive rivalry at WrestleDream in October 2023 had spiraled into a full-on war when Strickland took things too far. Before the night unfolded, the storylines had been brewing on AEW's flagship programs—Dynamite, Collision, and Rampage. Wrestling is always about the build, and AEW delivered it in spades this year. Feuds weren't just about the in-ring action—they were about redemption, unfinished business, and the chance to claim ultimate glory.

In one of the most personal rivalries, "Hangman" Adam Page and Swerve Strickland had been feuding for nearly a year. What began as a competitive rivalry at WrestleDream in October 2023 had spiraled into a full-on war when Strickland took things too far.

Strickland's shocking invasion of Page's home, entering his child's room while the family slept, turned a simple feud into a bitter, heated contest. Strickland won the earlier encounters, but Page, driven by rage and a thirst for revenge, was ready to finally get his hands on Swerve in a match that would be unlike any other—an Unsanctioned Lights Out Steel Cage Match.

Another significant storyline revolved around Bryan Danielson. Coming off a victory at All In, where Danielson retained his AEW World Championship, he was ready for his next challenge. Enter Jack Perry, whose ambition had no boundaries. Perry, who had pinned Danielson in a chaotic Anarchy in the Arena match, challenged him for the title at All Out. Danielson, ever the fighting champion, accepted.

Meanwhile, the AEW International Championship scene was just as electric. Will Ospreay, having regained his title at All In, was ready to defend it against a challenger he knew all too well—Pac, who had earned the title match at Global Glory Four-Way. The fight would take the crowd on a rollercoaster of high-flying action.

And in the mix of it all, AEW saw a brewing rivalry between MJF and Daniel Garcia, which reached its boiling point. After MJF made his surprise return from injury, he initially offered Garcia a helping hand—but their partnership crumbled when MJF turned on him. Now, Garcia had the chance to prove himself in a one-on-one match at All Out.

The Matches Begin

The excitement started early with the Zero Hour pre-show, where wrestling action kicked off with intensity. The Acclaimed, with their signature style, took on the Iron Savages, and in a hard-fought match, Bowens and Caster delivered their trademark moves to seal the win. It was clear from the start that the fans were in for a thrilling night.

Next, Sammy Guevara and Dustin Rhodes joined forces with Hologram to face The Premier Athletes (Tony Nese, Ari Daivari, and Josh Woods). With high-flying maneuvers and explosive finishes, Guevara and Rhodes took control, ultimately putting away Woods for the victory.

Following that, the Bang Bang Gang (Austin and Colten Gunn, Juice Robinson) took on the Dark Order

(Evil Uno, Alex Reynolds, John Silver), with the Bang Bang Gang emerging victorious after Robinson hit Uno with his signature Juice is Loose finishing move.

The final pre-show match saw a high-octane Three-Way Tag Team Match between The Undisputed Kingdom (Matt Taven, Mike Bennett, and Roderick Strong), The Beast Mortos and Shane Taylor Promotions, and Action Andretti and Top Flight. Strong would eventually get the pin on Andretti, a victory that sent a message to the AEW locker room: The Undisputed Kingdom was on the rise.

The Main Show

When the main card began, the energy in the arena was palpable. The first contest saw MJF face off against Daniel Garcia. Garcia, who had been humiliated by MJF for weeks, ambushed him before the bell rang. The match was hard-hitting, but in the end, MJF delivered a low blow, rolled Garcia up, and secured the win. The tension didn't end there—MJF extended his hand in a show of sportsmanship, only to land another low blow to Garcia before he brutally attacked him, leaving Garcia to recover in the stands.

Next, the AEW World Tag Team Championship was on the line, with The Young Bucks defending their titles against the Blackpool Combat Club duo, Claudio Castagnoli and Wheeler Yuta. The Young Bucks, ever the resilient champions, retained their titles after a surprising counter to BCC's signature Fast Ball Special. The match was as intense as it was strategic, with both teams showing why they were the best in AEW.

In one of the night's most highly anticipated matches, Will Ospreay defended his AEW International Championship against Pac. Ospreay hit all of his high-flying moves, including the Hidden Blade and Os-Cutter, to successfully defend his title against the unyielding Pac.

Then came the Chicago Street Fight, where Kris Statlander faced off against Willow Nightingale. The two women went to war, using every weapon they could find. Statlander picked up the win, delivering a tombstone piledriver on Nightingale, who had no choice but to submit after Statlander wrapped a chain around her face.

The Climactic Steel Cage Match

The night reached its peak in the main event. Hangman Adam Page and Swerve Strickland stepped into the steel cage for a battle like no other. The steel cage came to life as the two men fought with everything they had. The tools of destruction—staple guns, cinder blocks, steel chairs—were used to brutal effect. In the end, Page drove a hypodermic needle through Strickland's cheek and crushed his head with a steel chair, earning the knockout victory in a match that would be remembered for years to come.

Results

Zero Hour Matches:
1. The Acclaimed defeated Iron Savages by pinfall
2. Sammy Guevara & Dustin Rhodes defeated The Premier Athletes by pinfall
3. Bang Bang Gang defeated The Dark Order by pinfall
4. Undisputed Kingdom defeated Shane Taylor Promotions & Action Andretti & Top Flight by pinfall

Main Show Matches:
5. MJF defeated Daniel Garcia by pinfall
6. The Young Bucks defeated Blackpool Combat Club by pinfall
7. Will Ospreay defeated Pac by pinfall
8. Kris Statlander defeated Willow Nightingale by submission
9. Bryan Danielson defeated Jack Perry by pinfall
10. Hangman Adam Page defeated Swerve Strickland by knockout

This marks the end of the All Out 2024 event, an unforgettable night in AEW history. The rivalries were settled, the champions retained, and the foundation for future battles was laid. AEW fans would undoubtedly be talking about this night for years to come.

CHAPTER TWO

CHAPTER TWO
Wrestle-Dream 2024: A Night of Triumph and Heartbreak

Wrestle-Dream 2024: A Night of Triumph and Heartbreak

The Tacoma Dome in Tacoma, Washington, set the stage for AEW's WrestleDream 2024 event on October 12, 2024. This was no ordinary event. It wasn't just about the action inside the ring—it was a tribute, a celebration of the legacy of the legendary Antonio Inoki, the founder of New Japan Pro-Wrestling (NJPW), who had passed away on October 1, 2022. AEW had promised to honor him, and this night was destined to be a fitting tribute to the man who dreamed of wrestling uniting the world.

It was the second annual Wrestle-Dream, and AEW's partnership with NJPW had brought together the best talent from across the globe. The energy in the Tacoma Dome was electric. Fans had traveled from all over to witness an event that would honor Inoki's vision, and to see some of the biggest names in professional wrestling square off in high-stakes battles.

The Road to Wrestle-Dream

Before the event kicked off, the feuds and rivalries that had been brewing for months came to a head. Wrestlers were not only fighting for championship gold, but for pride, respect, and legacy.

The night's most emotional moment would undoubtedly be the AEW World Championship match between Jon Moxley and Bryan Danielson. Moxley had defeated Danielson at Wrestle-Dream 2023, but their rivalry continued to heat up.

Before the event kicked off, the feuds and rivalries that had been brewing for months came to a head. Wrestlers were not only fighting for championship gold, but for pride, respect, and legacy.

The night's most emotional moment would undoubtedly be the AEW World Championship match between Jon Moxley and Bryan Danielson. Moxley had defeated Danielson at WrestleDream 2023, but their rivalry continued to heat up. . Danielson's reign as champion had been hard-fought, but his time was running out. As the weeks went on, Moxley and Danielson would continue to clash, with the stakes being higher than ever. This match would decide not just who held the belt, but who would claim the ultimate victory in a bitter, longstanding rivalry.

Another focal point was Konosuke Takeshita's rise. The AEW International Championship match would see him face off against both Will Ospreay and Ricochet in a high-flying, chaotic three-way match. Takeshita was gaining momentum, and his partnership with Don Callis only made him more dangerous.

But perhaps one of the most anticipated feuds was the clash between Jay White and "Hangman" Adam Page. White had spent weeks taunting Page, and their animosity only intensified as the match approached. It wasn't just about victory—it was about proving who was the better man in the eyes of the fans.

The Night Begins: Zero Hour

The Zero Hour pre-show was filled with exciting, fast-paced action, setting the stage for what was to come in the main event.The Zero Hour pre-show was filled with exciting, fast-paced action, setting the stage for what was to come in the main event.

The first match saw Brian Cage challenge Atlantis Jr. for the ROH World Television Championship. The two powerhouse athletes went to war, with Cage hitting his signature Drill Claw to claim victory and win the title. Fans cheered as Cage's dominance continued to grow in AEW.

Following that, Anna Jay faced Harley Cameron in a battle between two rising stars. Jay hit her signature Glory Bomb for the victory, establishing herself as a force to be reckoned with in the women's division.

Then came the tag team excitement. The Acclaimed (Anthony Bowens and Max Caster), with Billy Gunn in their corner, squared off against MxM Collection (Mansoor and Mason Madden). The match was a showcase of athleticism, and after Bowens took out both opponents on the outside, Caster hit his Mic Drop finishing move on Mansoor for the win.

The final match of the Zero Hour pre-show was an intense Eight-Man Tag Team Match. The Conglomeration (Orange Cassidy and Kyle O'Reilly) and The Outrunners (Turbo Floyd and Truth Magnum) faced off against The Dark Order and The Premier Athletes.

With both teams fighting hard, it was The Outrunners who sealed the win, performing a neckbreaker and powerslam combination on Ariya Daivari.

The Main Show: High Stakes and Unforgettable Moments

As the main show began, the atmosphere in the Tacoma Dome shifted into overdrive. The opening match saw Jay White, accompanied by his partner Juice Robinson, take on "Hangman" Adam Page. It was a back-and-forth battle, with both men pulling out all the stops. Ultimately, White countered Page's Buckshot Lariat into his own devastating Blade Runner, securing the victory. White's cocky celebration was met with boos, while Page's frustration grew, knowing his journey was far from over.

In the next match, Mariah May defended her AEW Women's Championship against Willow Nightingale. May showed off her agility and strength, landing a stunning avalanche hurricanrana followed by her signature Storm Zero to keep Nightingale down for the three-count, retaining her title.

Then came the AEW TNT Championship match. Jack Perry faced Katsuyori Shibata, in a fight that had fans on the edge of their seats. Shibata's brutal strikes nearly took Perry out, but Perry managed to roll Shibata up for the pin after a back-and-forth struggle, retaining his championship.

The Ultimate Climax: Title Matches and Career-Defining Moments

As the night went on, the tension only grew. The AEW International Championship match was a highlight of the evening, with Will Ospreay, the defending champion, taking on both Ricochet and Konosuke Takeshita.

This was a match full of breathtaking aerial maneuvers and high-impact moments. After a series of brutal spots, Takeshita hit Ospreay with a knee strike, but it was Kyle Fletcher—hidden in a hoodie—who revealed himself as the true catalyst for the win. Fletcher attacked Ospreay with a Screwdriver, allowing Takeshita to secure the victory and claim the title.

Backstage, tensions boiled over as MJF confronted Daniel Garcia and Roderick Strong. The hostility was palpable, and it was clear that this would be far from over.

The Two-out-of-Three Falls Match between Hologram and The Beast Mortos was a brutal contest that saw both men exchange power moves. In the end, Hologram triumphed after a devastating super hurricanrana, taking the win in the decisive third fall.

The Ultimate Victory

Finally, the night ended with an unforgettable AEW World Championship match between Bryan Danielson and Jon Moxley. It was a grueling contest with both men pushing their bodies to the limit. Moxley, with his hard-hitting style and unrelenting aggression, took advantage of Danielson's fatigue, locking him in a sleeper hold to claim the victory and the championship.

As Danielson passed out, his career as a full-time wrestler came to a painful end.

After the match, Moxley and his group, The Death Riders, showed no mercy. They attacked Danielson, attempting to suffocate him with a plastic bag, but Darby Allin and Wheeler Yuta came to his rescue. However, their attempt to help Danielson was futile, as Moxley's stablemates held them back, leaving Danielson for dead.

Results

Zero Hour Matches:
1. Brian Cage defeated Atlantis Jr. by pinfall – ROH World Television Championship
2. Anna Jay defeated Harley Cameron by pinfall
3. The Acclaimed defeated MxM Collection by pinfall
4. The Outrunners defeated The Dark Order & The Premier Athletes by pinfall

Main Show Matches:
5. Jay White defeated "Hangman" Adam Page by pinfall
6. Mariah May defeated Willow Nightingale by pinfall – AEW Women's World Championship
7. Jack Perry defeated Katsuyori Shibata by pinfall – AEW TNT Championship
8. Konosuke Takeshita defeated Will Ospreay and Ricochet by pinfall – AEW International Championship
9. Hologram defeated The Beast Mortos 2-1 – Two-out-of-Three Falls Match
10. Jon Moxley defeated Bryan Danielson by technical submission – AEW World Championship

With the Wrestle-Dream 2024 event, AEW honored the legacy of Antonio Inoki while creating new moments that will go down in history. Champions were crowned, legacies were made, and some careers came to a close. The night belonged to those who fought for their place in AEW's bright future.

CHAPTER THREE

CHAPTER THREE
Full Gear 2024: The Ultimate Showdown

Full Gear 2024: The Ultimate Showdown

The atmosphere was electric on November 23, 2024, as the Prudential Center in Newark, New Jersey became the battlefield for AEW's Full Gear 2024. This was AEW's sixth annual Full Gear pay-per-view event, and it promised to deliver a night of heart-pounding action, shocking moments, and intense rivalries. This event was not just about the championship gold; it was about personal pride, redemption, and the opportunity for wrestlers to carve their names in the history books.

Full Gear had grown to become one of AEW's most prestigious events, and this year, it was poised to be one of the biggest shows in the promotion's history. The excitement in the arena was palpable as fans eagerly awaited the battles that would unfold. With major title defenses, long-brewing feuds coming to a head, and shocking twists in the storylines, there was no way to predict what was about to happen.

As the night drew closer, AEW had stacked the card with talent, promising not just great wrestling, but matches that would keep fans on the edge of their seats. The stage was set, the stars were ready, and the energy was undeniable. Let's take a look at the events that made this night unforgettable.

The Road to Full Gear

Before the action even began, the feuds and storylines that had been months in the making were about to explode. Jon Moxley, one of AEW's toughest competitors, had defended the AEW World Championship against some of the best wrestlers in the business.

But the true test of his reign would come when he faced Orange Cassidy, who had earned his title shot after an emotional journey of triumph and heartache. Cassidy was no stranger to Moxley's brutal fighting style, and the stage was set for a war.

Elsewhere, Bobby Lashley, the powerhouse from WWE, had made his AEW debut earlier in the year and quickly asserted his dominance. But his path to glory was interrupted by Swerve Strickland, a rising star with a chip on his shoulder. The two were set to meet in a contest that was as much about pride as it was about the gold on the line. Swerve had something to prove, and Lashley was determined to show the world that he was the true dominant force.

In the TNT Championship picture, Daniel Garcia had fought his way through the ranks to earn a chance to challenge Jack Perry, the reigning champion. The animosity between Garcia and Perry had been bubbling for months, with Perry recently attacking Garcia in a shocking move that pushed their rivalry to new heights. Garcia, having finally come into his own, was ready to claim the title.

One of the most anticipated moments of the night was the continuation of the bitter rivalry between MJF and Roderick Strong. MJF, the cocky and controversial champion, had proven time and again that he was willing to do whatever it took to hold on to his title. But Strong, with his unwavering determination and technical skill, was the perfect challenger. The match had the potential to steal the show, as both men were locked in a bitter battle for supremacy.

And of course, Mercedes Moné was set to defend her AEW TBS Championship against the tough challenger Kris Statlander. Statlander had already proven herself to be a formidable opponent, and the stakes were high for both women as they prepared for a no-holds-barred contest that could change the landscape of the women's division.

Zero Hour: The Pre-show Action

The excitement started before the main event even began with the Zero Hour pre-show. This event, while often overlooked by casual fans, had become an essential part of AEW's storytelling. It was a chance to see up-and-coming stars, as well as established names, do battle in intense matches that set the tone for the evening ahead.

The night kicked off with Deonna Purrazzo facing off against Anna Jay. Purrazzo, known for her technical prowess, fought with precision and control. But Jay, with her unyielding resilience, rolled Purrazzo up for the win in a shocking reversal, setting the tone for an unpredictable night.

Next, the action ramped up with a four-way match between Dante Martin, The Beast Mortos, Komander, and Buddy Matthews. The match was a fast-paced, high-flying spectacle, with all four competitors showcasing their incredible athleticism. In the end, Matthews would hit a devastating diving footstomp on Martin, claiming the victory in what was a thrilling start to the evening.

Then, in an unexpected moment of chaos, Big Boom! "A.J." and his son Big Justice squared off against QT Marshall in a highly anticipated match. With The Rizzler acting as the special guest timekeeper, the match had more than just a wrestling story to tell. A wild distraction and a powerbomb from A.J. gave him the victory, much to the delight of the fans who were cheering for the unlikely hero.

Main Show: High Stakes and Epic Feuds

As the main event began, the stakes had never been higher. The AEW World Championship was on the line in a brutal battle between the champion Jon Moxley and the fan-favorite Orange Cassidy. The match was a war, with Moxley using his hard-hitting style to wear down Cassidy. But Cassidy, known for his never-give-up attitude, fought back with everything he had. The match reached its peak when Moxley managed to lock Cassidy in a submission hold, forcing him to tap out and retain his title.

In a highly anticipated TBS Championship match, Mercedes Moné successfully defended her title against Kris Statlander. The two women went to war, with Moné's aggressive style contrasting against Statlander's sheer power. The match was hard-hitting, and after a brutal sequence of moves, Moné hit her finishing Moné Maker to retain her title.

The TNT Championship match between Jack Perry and Daniel Garcia was a hard-fought, emotional affair. Garcia, looking to prove himself, brought his A-game against Perry. But Perry, using his resilience and grit, hit a devastating Perry Bomb to retain his title in a match that had the crowd on the edge of their seats.

One of the night's most anticipated matches was the AEW International Championship contest between Konosuke Takeshita and Ricochet. Takeshita, with his newfound alliance with Don Callis, had the upper hand in the match. The two men delivered an unbelievable performance, with Ricochet's aerial skills and Takeshita's hard-hitting style keeping the fans on their feet. Takeshita would eventually pin Ricochet after a brutal Knee Strike, winning the title.

The Full Gear 2024 event also featured a Tag Team Championship match, with Private Party defending against the challengers Kings of the Black Throne (Malakai Black and Brody King). The match was a showcase of tag team excellence, but in the end, Private Party retained their titles in a fast-paced encounter that kept the fans on their toes.

The Main Event: MJF vs. Roderick Strong

Finally, the night came to a head with the most anticipated match: MJF defending his AEW World Championship against the hard-hitting Roderick Strong. Both men had spent months in the buildup to this moment, with Strong trying to prove that he was the true leader of AEW, while MJF, with his characteristic arrogance, had dismissed him at every turn. The match was a brutal affair, with both competitors taking their bodies to the limit. MJF, however, used every trick in his book, including some sneaky tactics, to finally submit Strong and retain his title.

Results

Zero Hour Matches:
1. Anna Jay defeated Deonna Purrazzo by pinfall
2. Buddy Matthews defeated Dante Martin, Komander, and The Beast Mortos by pinfall
3. Big Boom! "A.J." defeated QT Marshall by pinfall

Main Show Matches:
1. Jon Moxley defeated Orange Cassidy by submission – AEW World Championship
2. Mercedes Moné defeated Kris Statlander by pinfall – AEW TBS Championship
3. Jack Perry defeated Daniel Garcia by pinfall – AEW TNT Championship
4. Konosuke Takeshita defeated Ricochet by pinfall – AEW International Championship
5. Private Party defeated Kings of the Black Throne by pinfall – AEW World Tag Team Championship
6. MJF defeated Roderick Strong by submission – AEW World Championship

With the final bell, Full Gear 2024 came to a close, but the night's drama and emotions would echo in the minds of AEW fans for months to come. New champions were crowned, personal vendettas were settled, and the stakes were raised for the next chapter in AEW's thrilling story.

CHAPTER FOUR

CHAPTER FOUR
AEW Women's World Championship

AEW Women's World Championship

The AEW Women's World Championship is a prestigious title created and promoted by All Elite Wrestling (AEW), a professional wrestling organization in the United States. Established on October 2, 2019, the inaugural champion was Riho. The title is currently held by Mariah May, who claimed her first reign by defeating "Timeless" Toni Storm at All In on August 25, 2024, in London, England.

History

AEW President Tony Khan announced plans for a women's singles and tag team championship on June 18, 2019, six months after the promotion was established. Chief Brand Officer Brandi Rhodes later revealed that the AEW Women's World Championship belt would debut at All Out on August 31, 2019, and the first champion would be crowned during the inaugural broadcast of AEW Dynamite on October 2.

The contenders for the inaugural championship match were determined at All Out. Nyla Rose earned her spot by winning the women's Casino Battle Royale during the pre-show, while Riho defeated Hikaru Shida on the main card to secure her place. On the first episode of Dynamite, Riho defeated Rose to become the first AEW Women's World Champion.

Thunder Rosa, reigning champion in September 2022, was forced to withdraw from her title defense at All Out due to a back injury. Rather than vacate the title, an interim champion was crowned.

Toni Storm emerged victorious in a four-way match, defeating Dr. Britt Baker, Jamie Hayter, and Hikaru Shida. Later, Hayter defeated Storm at Full Gear to claim the interim championship. On November 23, Rosa officially relinquished her title, making Hayter the undisputed champion and retroactively recognizing Storm's interim reign as official.

Belt Design

The original AEW Women's World Championship belt featured a small oval-shaped center plate with three side plates on each side. The center plate displayed a crown at the top, decorative edges, and a nameplate for the reigning champion's name. Above the nameplate was the AEW logo, while "Women's World Wrestling Champion" appeared below. Gold and nickel plates adorned the black leather strap.

On May 28, 2021, a revised version of the belt was unveiled to commemorate Hikaru Shida's record-setting 370-day reign. The updated belt maintained the original design but featured a larger size, additional encrusted diamonds, and extra gold plating. The side plates were reduced from three to two on each side. However, Shida lost the title two days later to Dr. Britt Baker at Double or Nothing.

At Revolution on March 6, 2022, Baker introduced a new design featuring larger gold plates on a black strap. The center plate depicted a globe highlighting North and South America, with banners reading "Women's World" above and "Wrestling Champion" below. The AEW logo adorned the top of the plate, with intricate filigree filling the remaining space. This version omitted the nameplate present in earlier designs.

The inner side plates showcased sections of the globe not displayed on the center plate, while the outer side plates featured two wrestlers grappling beneath the AEW logo. Designed by Andre Dorsey, the belt took three weeks to complete and was inspired by the Mid-South North American Championship of the 1980s.

Reigns

As of December 19, 2024, the AEW Women's World Championship has been held by nine champions across 13 reigns, with one vacancy. Riho was the inaugural champion, while Hikaru Shida and "Timeless" Toni Storm are tied for the most reigns at three each. Shida holds records for the longest reign (372 days), the shortest reign (25 days), and the longest combined reign (435 days). Nyla Rose is the oldest champion, winning at age 37, while Riho remains the youngest, claiming the title at age 22.

Mariah May is the current champion, having won her first reign by defeating Toni Storm at All In on August 25, 2024. As of December 19, 2024, her reign has surpassed 116 recognized days.

Cumulative Reigns

Hikaru Shida leads with a combined 436 days across three reigns, followed closely by Toni Storm with 423 days. Dr. Britt Baker, Jamie Hayter, Thunder Rosa, Riho, Mariah May, Nyla Rose, and Saraya round out the list of champions with varying reign durations. Notably, Shida's first reign of 372 days remains unmatched in AEW's history.

CHAPTER FIVE

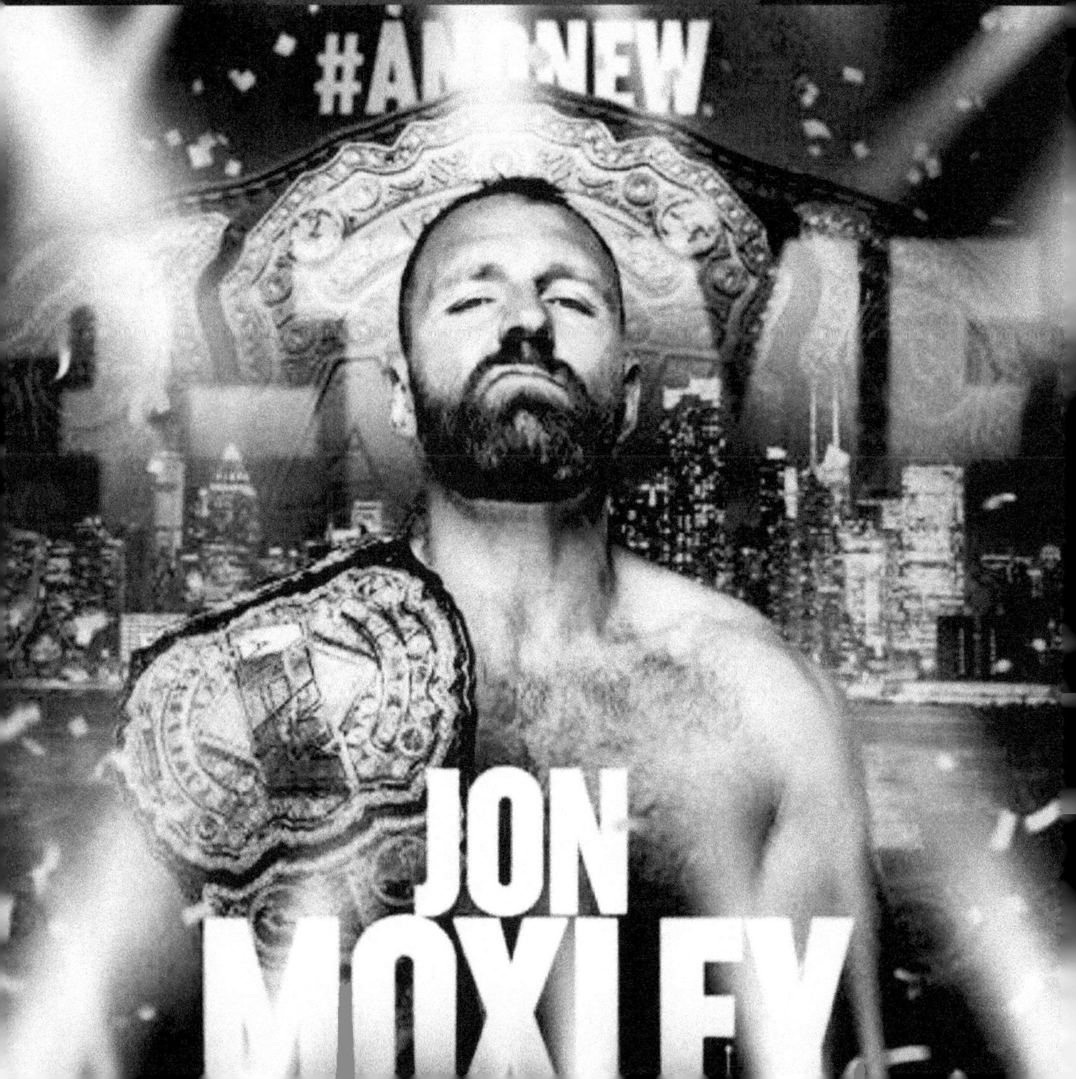

#ANDNEW

JON MOXLEY

CHAPTER FIVE
AEW World Championship

AEW World Championship

The AEW World Championship stands as the premier title in All Elite Wrestling (AEW), an American professional wrestling promotion. Introduced on May 25, 2019, it is recognized as AEW's most prestigious accolade. Chris Jericho was the first to claim the title, setting the standard for the championship's legacy. Currently, Jon Moxley holds the belt, marking his record-breaking fourth reign. He secured the championship by defeating Bryan Danielson at WrestleDream on October 12, 2024.

History

AEW's formation on January 1, 2019, marked a new chapter in professional wrestling. Its first major event, Double or Nothing, was scheduled for May 25. Days before, a humorous video on AEW's YouTube channel featured actor Jack Whitehall attempting to unveil the championship but struggling with its bag. The video revealed that the Casino Battle Royale winner at Double or Nothing's pre-show would later face the main event victor to determine the first champion. AEW president Tony Khan clarified that the championship would not follow weight divisions, though it has occasionally been referred to as a heavyweight title.

At Double or Nothing, "Hangman" Adam Page won the Casino Battle Royale, while Chris Jericho triumphed over Kenny Omega in the main event, setting the stage for the inaugural championship match. Wrestling legend Bret Hart revealed the title belt during the event, and the championship was later contested at AEW's All Out on August 31.

Jericho defeated Page to become the first AEW World Champion. However, the title belt was stolen shortly after and recovered within days.

A significant moment came on June 3, 2022, when CM Punk, recently crowned champion, announced an injury that required surgery. Rather than vacating the title, AEW introduced an interim championship. This led to the AEW Interim World Championship Eliminator Series, culminating at AEW x NJPW: Forbidden Door. Jon Moxley emerged as the interim champion by defeating Hiroshi Tanahashi. Punk later returned but lost to Moxley in a unification match.

Controversy arose at All Out in September 2022, when Punk regained the title but became embroiled in a backstage altercation with AEW executives. This led to his suspension and the championship's vacancy. A tournament at Grand Slam crowned Jon Moxley as the new champion, marking his third reign.

"Real World Championship"

CM Punk reignited discussions upon his return to AEW on June 17, 2023, unveiling the championship belt he never lost. Declaring himself the "real world's champion," he marked the title with a symbolic black X. Though unofficial, Punk defended the belt until his contract was terminated following an incident at All In on August 27, effectively ending the "Real World Championship."

Belt Design

The AEW World Championship features a black leather strap with five plates in silver and gold. The central plate showcases the AEW logo with banners reading "WORLD" and "CHAMPION" above and below, flanked by globe motifs. Initially, the side plates featured AEW's logo and globe halves. After Samoa Joe's victory on December 30, 2023, the belt was updated to include customizable inner side plates for each champion's logo, akin to WWE designs.

Custom Designs

Notable customizations include MJF's "Big Burberry Belt," introduced on November 30, 2022, featuring a brown strap with Burberry's signature pattern. On December 29, 2023, AEW president Tony Khan gifted a custom belt to Clemson University's football coach, celebrating their Gator Bowl victory. The belt featured the Tigers' logo and event details.

Reigns

As of December 19, 2024, the AEW World Championship has seen 13 reigns among nine champions, with one vacancy and an interim titleholder. MJF's reign of 406 days is the longest, while Punk's second reign lasted just three days. Jericho became the oldest champion at 48 years old, and MJF the youngest at 26. Jon Moxley, now in his fourth reign, claimed his latest victory over Bryan Danielson at WrestleDream in Tacoma, Washington.

CHAPTER SIX

CHAPTER SIX
AEW International Championship

AEW International Championship

The AEW International Championship, created by All Elite Wrestling (AEW), is a secondary title for male wrestlers. Unlike AEW's primary championships, this title is unique in being defended not only on AEW programming but also in promotions worldwide. Initially established as the AEW All-Atlantic Championship on June 8, 2022, the title was rebranded to the International Championship on March 15, 2023. Currently, Konosuke Takeshita holds the title in his first reign, which he claimed on October 12, 2024, by defeating Ricochet and former champion Will Ospreay in a three-way match at WrestleDream.

History

The AEW International Championship was introduced during the June 8, 2022, episode of Dynamite as the AEW All-Atlantic Championship. It was intended to represent AEW fans globally, with no specific focus on the Atlantic Ocean or surrounding nations. The inaugural champion was crowned at the Forbidden Door pay-per-view on June 26, 2022, a joint event with New Japan Pro-Wrestling (NJPW). Six qualifying matches determined the four competitors for the championship bout: Pac, Miro, and Malakai Black represented AEW, while NJPW's Clark Connors replaced Tomohiro Ishii due to injury. Pac emerged victorious, submitting Connors to become the first champion.

AEW President Tony Khan emphasized the championship's unique appeal in an interview, highlighting that it would be defended internationally.

True to this vision, Pac defended the title in promotions such as Revolution Pro Wrestling (RevPro) in the UK, Over the Top Wrestling (OTT) in Ireland, NJPW in Japan, Consejo Mundial de Lucha Libre (CMLL) in Mexico, and Maple Leaf Pro Wrestling (MLP) in Canada. His reign lasted 108 days, the second longest in the title's history.

In March 2023, AEW rebranded the championship to the International Championship, aligning the change with the premiere of Shazam! Fury of the Gods, as part of AEW's partnership with Warner Bros. During this transition, Orange Cassidy retained the title and became both the final All-Atlantic Champion and the first International Champion. Cassidy's reign, lasting an unprecedented 326 days, remains the longest in the title's history, with a total of 471 days across his two reigns.

The championship temporarily took on a new identity during MJF's reign in July 2024, when he unofficially renamed it the "AEW American Championship." MJF introduced a custom belt design reflecting his vision but lost the title to Will Ospreay at All In on August 25, 2024, leading to the restoration of the International Championship name.

Belt Design

The original design, crafted by Ron Edwardsen of Red Leather Belts, featured a central globe surrounded by flags representing Mexico, China, the UK, the US, Canada, and Japan. AEW's logo sat above the globe, with "All-Atlantic" on a banner above and "Champion" on a banner below.

Two side plates on each side of the center plate showcased either wrestlers in action or AEW's logo above a globe.

When the championship was rebranded in 2023, the "All-Atlantic" banner was replaced with "International." During MJF's reign, a custom version of the belt included an American flag-inspired strap, a map of the contiguous US in place of the globe, and satirical inscriptions on the side plates targeting the UK and Will Ospreay. This design was retired when Ospreay reclaimed the title at All In.

Reigns

Since its inception, the AEW International Championship has seen ten reigns among eight champions. Pac was the inaugural titleholder, while Orange Cassidy and Will Ospreay are tied for the most reigns at two each. Cassidy's first reign remains the longest at 326 days, while Jon Moxley's reign of just 17 days is the shortest. Roderick Strong is the oldest champion, winning at age 40, and MJF is the youngest, securing the title at 28.

The current champion, Konosuke Takeshita, claimed his first reign by defeating Ricochet and Will Ospreay at WrestleDream on October 12, 2024. As of December 19, 2024, his reign has surpassed 68 days and continues to grow.

Legacy

The AEW International Championship has become a symbol of AEW's global reach, with its defenders showcasing the title across multiple countries and promotions. From Pac's groundbreaking victory to Cassidy's historic reign and MJF's controversial customization, the championship reflects the diverse talents and storylines that define AEW's innovative approach to professional wrestling.

CHAPTER SEVEN

CHAPTER SEVEN
AEW TBS Championship

AEW TBS Championship

The AEW TBS Championship is a secondary women's professional wrestling title introduced by All Elite Wrestling (AEW). Named after the TBS television network, which airs AEW's flagship program Dynamite, the championship was established on October 6, 2021, to elevate the women's division. Jade Cargill became the first champion, setting a high bar for the title's legacy. Currently, Mercedes Moné holds the title in her first reign, having defeated Willow Nightingale at Double or Nothing on May 26, 2024, in Paradise, Nevada.

History

The AEW TBS Championship was introduced in response to the successful establishment of the AEW TNT Championship for the men's division in 2020. With Dynamite set to move from TNT to TBS in January 2022, AEW announced plans for a women's television title to complement the network transition. On October 6, 2021, during the second-anniversary episode of Dynamite, AEW commentator Tony Schiavone and referee Aubrey Edwards formally unveiled the TBS Championship. AEW announced that the first champion would be determined through a 12-woman single-elimination tournament.

The tournament began on October 23, 2021, and concluded on January 5, 2022, coinciding with Dynamite's debut on TBS. Jade Cargill triumphed over Ruby Soho in the final to become the inaugural TBS Champion, cementing her place in AEW history with an unparalleled reign of 508 days.

Subsequent champions have added their own chapters to the title's story:
- Kris Statlander ended Cargill's historic reign at Double or Nothing on May 28, 2023.
- Julia Hart captured the title in a three-way bout at Full Gear on November 18, 2023, pinning Skye Blue.
- Willow Nightingale claimed the championship in a "House Rules" match on April 21, 2024, defeating Hart under stipulations that barred outside interference.
- Mercedes Moné defeated Nightingale at Double or Nothing 2024, beginning her first reign.

The TBS Championship Tournament

The TBS Championship Tournament featured a 12-woman bracket, starting with four first-round matches. Key moments in the tournament included:
- Jade Cargill pinning Red Velvet on November 17, 2021, to advance to the semifinals.
- Thunder Rosa defeating Jamie Hayter on December 29, 2021, in a grueling quarterfinal match, before falling to Ruby Soho in the semifinals.
- Ruby Soho defeating Kris Statlander in the quarterfinals and ultimately advancing to the final.

In the climactic bout on January 5, 2022, Jade Cargill defeated Ruby Soho to become the first champion, marking the beginning of her record-breaking reign.

Belt Design

The TBS Championship belt shares a similar design with the AEW TNT Championship, featuring a black leather strap and six plates. The centerpiece prominently displays the TBS network logo, with AEW's logo above it and a blue banner reading "CHAMPION" below.

The inner side plates highlight the historic "Tara on Techwood" building, which once housed TBS and TNT. The outer side plates display the AEW logo, while a smaller side plate on the far right also bears AEW's branding. The belt was designed by Red Leather and constructed by Rey Rey Championship Belts.

Reigns

As of December 19, 2024, the AEW TBS Championship has seen five champions across five reigns:

1. Jade Cargill: The inaugural champion reigned for an unprecedented 508 days, defeating Ruby Soho in the tournament final on January 5, 2022.
2. Kris Statlander: Cargill's reign ended when Statlander claimed the title on May 28, 2023, holding it for 174 days.
3. Julia Hart: Hart won the title at Full Gear on November 18, 2023, pinning Skye Blue in a three-way match.
4. Willow Nightingale: Nightingale defeated Hart on April 21, 2024, in a "House Rules" match with stipulations preventing interference.
5. Mercedes Moné: Moné claimed the championship at Double or Nothing on May 26, 2024, and continues her reign.

Legacy

Jade Cargill's record-breaking reign set a high standard for the TBS Championship, defining it as a cornerstone of AEW's women's division. Subsequent champions have built on her legacy, showcasing diverse styles and storylines. Mercedes Moné's current reign continues to elevate the championship, further solidifying its importance in professional wrestling.

Author Request

Dear fellow wrestling enthusiasts,

If, like me, you were carried away by the electrifying intensity of AEW's most spectacular year, then my newly released book, "LET ME TELL YOU THE Q4 STORY OF AEW IN 2024 TO BEGIN YOUR 2025," could be just up your alley. I've documented the heart-stopping near falls, gravity-defying moonsaults, and moments of pure treachery that left us all reeling from All Out, WrestleDream, Full Gear, AEW Women's World Championship, AEW World Championship, AEW International Championship and AEW TBS Championship in its pages.

The narrative, however, does not finish with me. Your voice, your point of view, will really bring this book to life. So, if you've been captivated by the tales weaved inside these pages, I sincerely beseech you to consider leaving a rating or perhaps writing a brief review.

Your comments, whether glowing or perceptive, will not only help me understand how my efforts were received by other fans, but will also take those on the fence into the thrilling world of AEW via your trusted lens.

Remember that every word, every star, and every click counts. So, if you've been enthralled by AEW's magnetism, please help me spread the news! Let's continue the discourse, one moonsault at a time.

Sincerely,
Your fellow traveler through the incredible journey that is AEW,
Jack Vale.

Additional Notes

"Want to dive deeper into the world of AEW and enhance your 2025 viewing experience?

The 'Additional Notes' page features exciting recommendations to fuel your fandom beyond the electrifying Q4 of 2024.

- Relive the Birth of AEW: Delve into my in-depth analysis of 'AEW All In 2023 Combined' and witness the historic event that ignited the AEW revolution.
- Explore the Best of 2023: Uncover the captivating stories and characters of the 'Best TV Shows of 2023 Compiled' and elevate your entertainment choices.
- Experience the Thrill of 2023: Relive the most electrifying moments of 'wrestling book of the year 2023' and prepare for another year of incredible wrestling action.
- Witness the Rise of AEW in 2024: Delve into 'aew all in 2024 compiled' and experience the continued evolution of All Elite Wrestling.

Don't miss these insightful reads!"

Do you want more? Go to [https://www.amazon.com/author/jackvale] to learn more or Scan QR Code below with a device.

You'll find all of my books there, as well as unique material, information on new projects, and even a platform to speak directly with me!

Let's keep the adventure going, friends!

Yours in stories and travels,

Jack Vale.

www.ingramcontent.com/pod-product-compliance
Lightning Source LLC
Chambersburg PA
CBHW070416230526
45471CB00006B/2831